Life lessons from Living with Luke

How my Autistic son is teaching me how to live better.

To Luke/Tiddles, who will never read this.

<u>*Introduction*</u>

I started blogging about the 'breakdown' of my relationship with my Autistic teenage son Luke in April 2013. I had become aware, albeit slowly, that he was drifting away from me both emotionally and physically. He no longer wanted to be near me, or even talk to me, going to such lengths as to shout at me and sometimes even physically attack me. However, as I have been writing, I began to notice certain things that keep cropping up from time to time. I originally started the blogs as a way of journaling my life with Tiddles, as I call him, and it brought to the surface a lot of feelings, hopes and fears that had been buried deep within me for over ten years since he had been diagnosed at age 2 and a half. I was finding that since he had reached 13, he had been taking a seemingly growing dislike to me and I couldn't figure out why. What I was finding was that he was taking out all of his frustrations and whatever else was going on in his little world, or Narnia as I called it in the blogs and venting it on me. I was quite happy to take the hits - rather me than his mum, his older brother, or anybody else for that matter, was my thinking behind it - and so I allowed him to carry on doing it. It ranged from slaps, punches, kicks, shouting, telling me to go away, sometimes not even acknowledging me in any way. And it hurt both physically and mentally.

But amongst the 'abuse' – and some people have called it that, although I personally do not see it as such - there were times when we would re-connect. Times when he was once again Luke, my little boy. I would get a glimpse of the son he might've been had Autism's shadow not fallen over him. And it was in these times that I would learn things from him about how to live. Strangely enough the more I looked, the more I found things to learn when he was smacking me as well.

So, I'd like to share with you the life lessons that my beautiful Autistic boy Tiddles, my Luke is trying to teach this 40-something Old Man.

Nothing lasts forever

Guess what? We're all going to die. It's a sad but true fact. It doesn't matter how much money you have or how many toys you own, how well you do or don't look after yourself, in the end you will end up with exactly what you came into this world with - nothing. And that's OK It really is. If you accept the fact that indeed, nothing lasts forever then you can go forward safe in the knowledge that all pain, all sadness, all everything will eventually pass. I have long since thought that my relationship with Tiddles was something that would last forever and a day. But I know that it won't. And whilst this does make me sad, it also makes me happy to know that he may well not like me much now, hopefully this too will pass. And this leads on nicely to…

<u>This too shall pass</u>

Because it will. It's similar to Nothing Lasts Forever in this respect, because as much as I wish certain things to last forever, I know deep in my heart that this too shall pass. I have had moments of deep despair, times when I have thought of just finishing everything and ending it all. But having this 'mantra' has taught me that it will all pass eventually. I have had bad times, and I have had times when I have been positively euphoric, almost as if I were on something that made me feel this good. But this too has passed. And if you have a sensible head on your shoulders, then just keep this in mind, that whatever you're experiencing right now...This Too Shall Pass.

(And that picture is meant to be blurry by the way...)

Stay strong

What is it that makes us strong? Is it physical strength? Emotional? To me, it's both. Tiddles has shown me – in his own autwisted way – that I need both, that I can't have one without the other. If I don't have the emotional strength to deal with his ever-increasing rejection of me, then I am going to crumble under the weight of the pain of his pushing me away. If I don't have the physical strength, then I'm going to get crushed by the sheer force of this whirling tornado of an already stocky teenager. One who is going to get bigger as he gets older and one who I am going to have to match to keep up with, if only to keep what little contact we have between us intact, however physically painful that is and may continue to be. This could be seen as 'tough love', being 'cruel to be kind', or any other cliché that you care to think of. I just think of it as 'life'. If I can deal with this, then surely I should be able to deal with anything, shouldn't I?

<u>Don't be afraid</u>

Tiddles appears to be fearless. The idea that you shouldn't be afraid comes from the notion that living with an autistic is somehow frightening. Daunting, certainly. Scary, possibly. But frightening? Well it depends on your point of view. If you view the whole world of Special Needs/ASD frightening, then naturally you are going to be frightened of the whole process. The thing is, it's not at all scary. Put yourself in the shoes of an autistic child. They are in a world - our world - where their senses are constantly assaulted by noise and stimulus from all around and whilst we have a natural inbuilt filter to block out a lot of the information and sounds being bombarded at us, Autistic children and indeed adults, do not have this luxury. They are perpetually being hit from all sides by pictures, sounds, music, noises of all sorts, traffic, etc. Is it any wonder that they sometimes have to curl up into a ball and hide? Sometimes I feel like doing that myself! It's a natural reaction when you think about it and something that we have done since childhood. Whenever things got too much for us then we would try and block out the sounds and squeeze our eyes tightly shut.

Usually during Doctor Who...

Live in the moment

Living in the moment is one of the easiest and also the most difficult thing to achieve. Why? Because there is so much going on around us these days, so many distractions. But if there is one thing that Tiddles has taught me, it's Living in the Moment. Tiddles doesn't appear to have any concept of time. To him it's all about the Now. What's happening NOW. Not what happened 5 minutes ago, not what happened yesterday, last week, last year...NOW. And only now. The upset he felt this morning has been replaced by the absolute joy of jumping around and watching his favourite current TV programme. And that is the way to live. Not having to worry about time. Or being governed by a clock in any way. It's beautiful to behold, because he is totally wrapped up in whatever he is doing in this moment. He and other beautiful autistic and Special Needs children and adults all Live In The Moment.

And it's wonderful.

<u>Not everybody loves you</u>

The painful truth of this is that, despite all of your best efforts, not everybody is going to love you. Worse than that, not everybody is going to even like you. In fact, some people will positively hate you. Sorry. That's the way of the world. You can't please all of the people, all of the time. If there is one thing I have learned from (sometimes physically) painful experience living with an autistic son, is that you will be kept on your toes with regards to your relationship together. I cannot explain it, nor can I understand it, but I have to accept it. Not everybody will love you. Don't be a people pleaser, because you will be fighting a losing battle, my friend. Even the most popular and famous people in the world, in history, didn't have the undying affection of every single person on the planet. It's impossible to achieve. So stop trying. As long as SOMEBODY loves you, then you are in a good place. It may not be the person that you WANT to love you, but...

Accept things

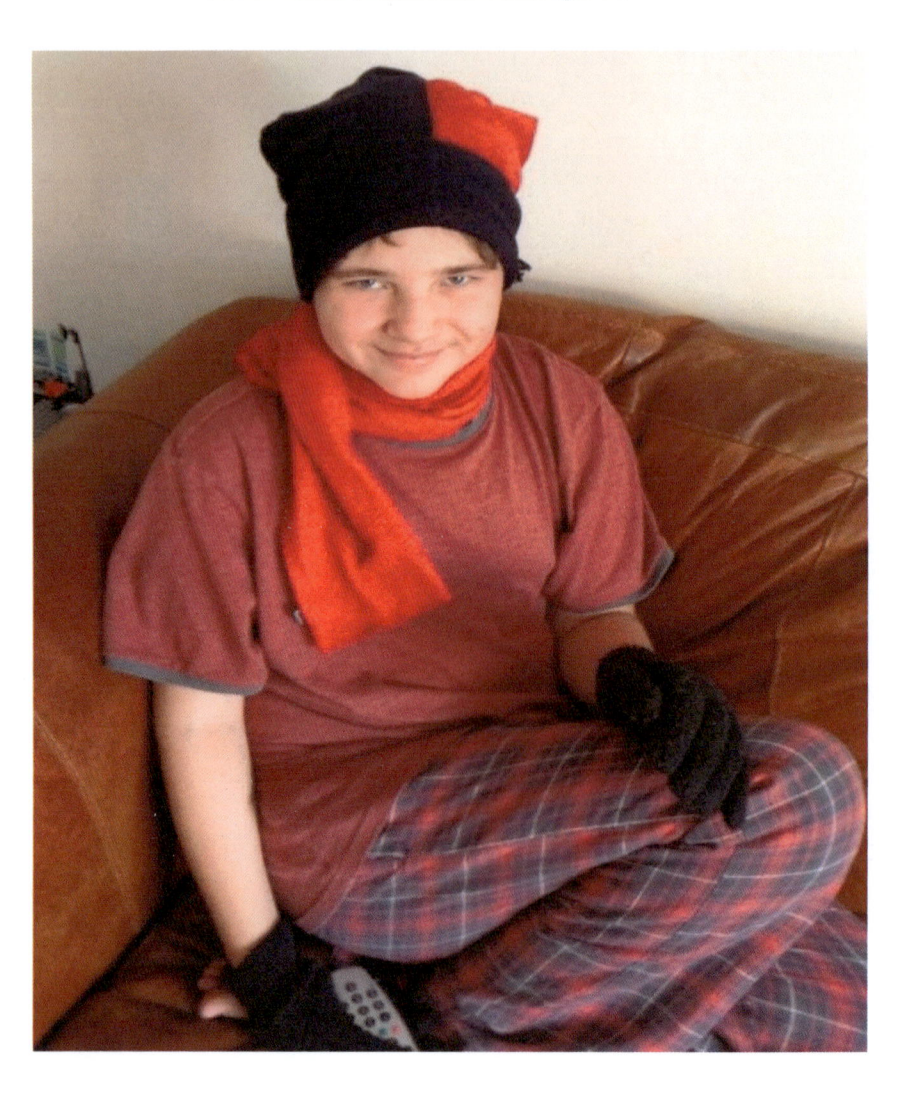

Now, if you can Accept Things, then you will live a better life. Now when I say accept things, I do not mean 'everything', because there are some things that you should never accept – rudeness, government policies, credit card charges, that Spurs will never win the Premiership (we live in hope...), but accept things that sometimes you just have no control over. Tiddles used to be a little boy. Now, as I write this, he is a 16 year old, hairy legged, brillo pad faced teenager. My little beautiful boy is gone. The boy who used to fall asleep on my chest has disappeared, to be replaced by a hulking, baritone voiced youth who now stands almost level with me. And I have to accept that. I mourn the boy that is gone, even though he is still here.

That part, when we had time together, has vanished, 'like tears in the rain...' Now I could, quite easily, allow myself the luxury of looking back and wishing the time over. But it's never going to happen, so I have to Accept it. Because otherwise I'll be looking back so much that I will miss the things that are happening now and they will then become the memories of tomorrow, and I'll be looking back at those too.

Spend time alone

Tiddles loves being on his own. The nature of his condition makes this practically a pre-requisite, a default state if you like. But even here, he is able to teach me/us something. He is comfortable in his own company. He knows how to occupy his time. Never will he state that he is bored and that he has nothing to do. Whether it be reading, running, playing with his trains, or even just digging a hole to sit in, he knows how to fill his busy day with important things that make him happy. To you or I, the mere act of digging a hole for no reason seems totally alien to us, let alone sitting in it for a while doing...nothing, except picking up mud and throwing it around. And indulging the whim of the amateur photographer of course.

But again, he's happy. He's occupied and he is showing the rest of us that even in these little things, there is a beauty almost in the simplicity of it all.

Now I know that the real world comes knocking with bills to pay, chores to do, meals to cook, etc, etc., yadda-yadda-yadda. But if you get even just a few minutes alone, take them, and do whatever you need to do that will make you happy.

Spend time with your family

So, whilst you should indeed spend time on your own, you should also spend time with family, whether it's your partner and/or children, or just your parents/brothers/sisters/etc...

Why? Because, if you're like me, then spending time with your family can sometimes bring several of these life lessons together at one time – especially 'Laugh'.

But how has Tiddles taught me about this? Simply by NOT spending time with me, he has made me appreciate more the importance of spending time with those people who DO actually want to spend time with me. I know that Tiddles will never have this little moment of clarity. He isn't ever going to wake up one day and think, *'That old man is not going to be here one day. I'd better start spending more time with him...'* And whilst I've never thought that about my own family, at least not in those terms, I have realised that Nothing Is Forever, and to spend even just 10 minutes with those who will one day will not even be there for one more minute, is just as important as spending a day with them.

He's not daft, that boy...

<u>Laugh</u>

And when I say laugh, I mean LAUGH. Laugh in an unbridled, carefree way as if you are the only person in the world. Laugh like your life depends on it. Laugh and risk dying of laughter. I personally have experienced moments of absolute hysterical laughter, where I have been unable to breathe, and they are incredible to experience. The power of laughter is often underestimated, but it's health benefits have long since been written about. Infectious as a cold and a lot more enjoyable, you have the power to make yourself feel better in an instant.

Don't believe me? Then go to the Living with Luke Facebook page and look for the video of Tiddles laughing. And if it doesn't make you at least smile, then your soul is dead...

That is how to laugh my friends...

If you want to jump, then jump

In other words, do whatever it is that you want to do at that particular moment in time...

And if you want to dress as a superhero, then do that...

If you want to jump, then jump...

If you want to eat three bowls of tomato soup, then do that...

And if you want to sing at the top of your voice in the supermarket, scaring old ladies when you do, then do that...

Accept gifts

This means not only physical gifts, but also emotional ones too. Tiddles appears not to actually like me. This subject has been open to debate for a few years now. But there are times when he will give me a wonderful gift. It could be time, and sometimes it's attention. He will spend maybe 5 minutes 'playing'. It could be re-enacting something from a TV show he's been watching - Scooby Doo or Batman usually - or it could be just him sitting with me, sometimes with his feet resting on my legs as he watches something on his iPad, or sometimes he actually sits on my lap. Now he's 16 years old and he's not a small lad, but even so I will quite happily let him sit where he wants to just because it happens so rarely and it's something that he, in his own little way, has decided that I need from him. And 9 times out of 10, I do.

And the other one time, I do as well.

Remember the past, but don't live in it

As I said previously, it's great sometimes to remember the past. And sometimes, it's not so great. There may have been times when you have been terribly hurt by something or someone and you cannot shake that memory for whatever reason. That's fine, just don't live in the past. The past is gone. It's not anything that you can do anything about now, except leave it where it is, in the past. The last minute has gone. You cannot get that back either.

So what can you do about it?

Nothing. Except live for the now. Tiddles does just that. The things that have already happened, have happened and not only does he not care about them now, he doesn't let it affect his present mood. If he wanted to then maybe he would, but his autism doesn't allow him that 'luxury' of retrospection, and he is probably the most authentic person I know and certainly somebody I can learn from.

Too often our minds are like butterflies, flitting from one subject to another, never fully engaging in what we are doing in that particular moment, always thinking about what we should be doing next. Tiddles does one thing, and only one thing, at a time. And then moves on to the next thing.

Now THAT is something we could all benefit from...

Find your own Narnia

Tiddles lives in Narnia. It's a safe haven for him, away from the world with all of it's noise and stresses. It's somewhere he goes to on a regular basis. It could be somewhere that you can go to in your mind, or it could actually be somewhere physical. It could be a forest, the beach, anywhere that makes you feel better.

Find yours.

We all need a Narnia, a fantasy land where we can have some private time to escape our daily lives, even if it is only for a few minutes. If we're lucky, we may be able to stay for longer, but stay for as long as you can before real life drags you back.

And if you're REALLY lucky, you may just find a wardrobe to disappear into...

<u>Don't look for approval</u>

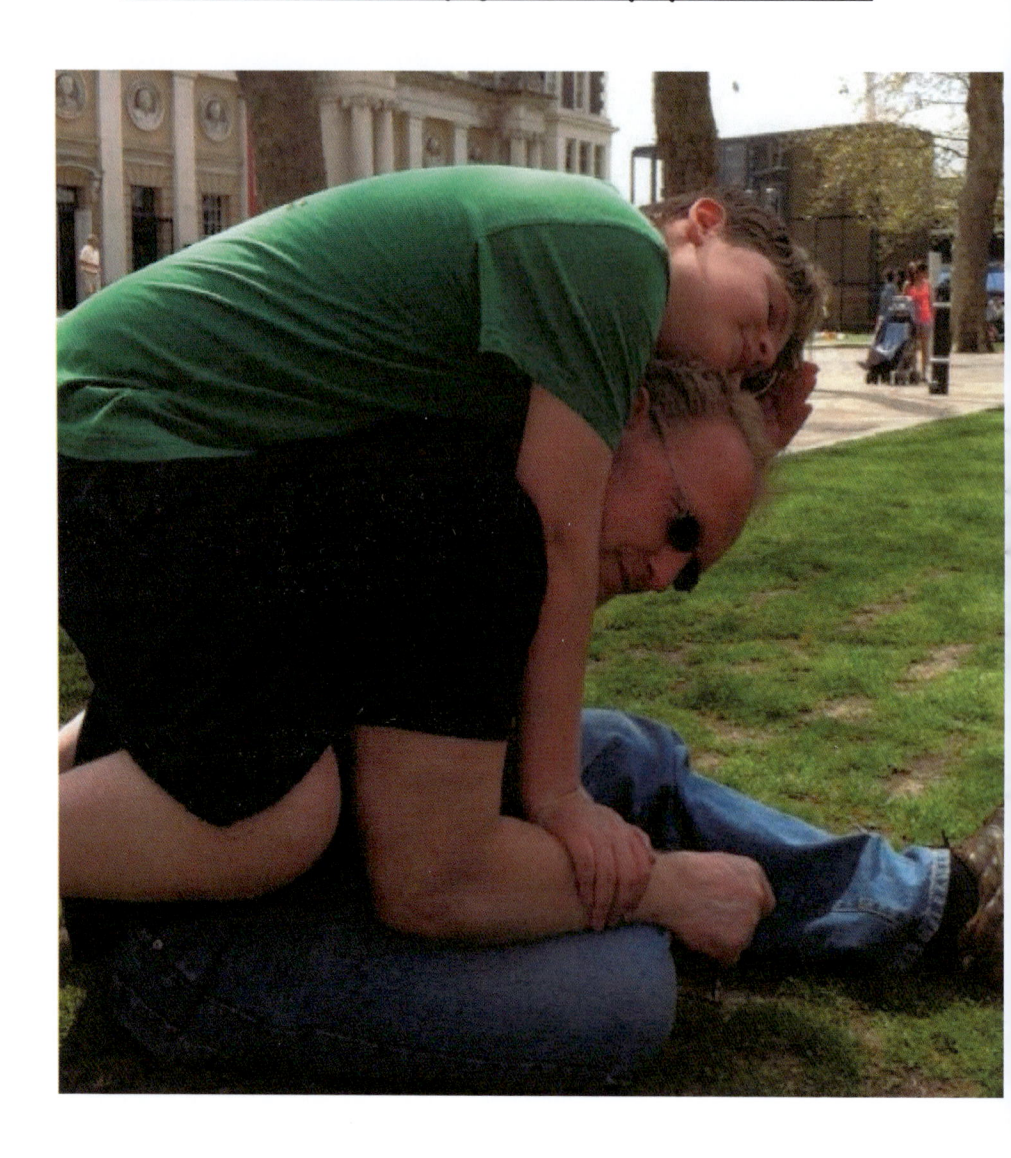

I have done the exact opposite of this for years, and continue to do so, so this is one of those lessons that are 'ongoing'. I have sought the approval of family, friends, teachers, children and adults alike, even strangers for crying out loud...

I have done things in the past, not because I really wanted to but solely so that people could look at me and think, *'Wow! That guy is really great...'*

Pathetic, really.

And then I look at Tiddles, who couldn't give a toss about seeking the approval of his own family, let alone the views of anybody else outside of his sanctuary.

It's not that he's a rule-breaker – he doesn't even know there are even rules to break – but he does have a view of the world that says, *'I'm going to do this...oh, you're applauding me? Well, could you kindly shut up, because I want to get on...'*

Praise, approval, plaudits, are just words. And words used by other people, not by Tiddles. He wouldn't know the meaning of them even if he did. They are as alien to him as a girlfriend. Doesn't need them, doesn't want them, wouldn't care about them if he did. They are just not important to him in his life. He does things for himself, and not for anybody else.

Unlike his stupid old man...

Don't wait

Probably the longest, hardest lesson of them all, and one I should've learned many, many years before Tiddles was even born, if I'm honest.

At the time of writing this, I am now 47 years old. I've waited too long to do a lot of things, and there are a lot of things that I regret not doing. And what it boils down to, is fear. Fear of failing, fear of losing everything and, bizarrely, fear of success. What Tiddles has shown me, is that really, you shouldn't have a plan. At least not when it comes to making decisions. As with If You Want To Jump, Then Jump, Tiddles doesn't tend to think of the consequences of his actions. He feels like doing something, so he goes right ahead and does it. If something gets broken then we deal with it IF it happens. Why worry about the IF, if IT never actually happens? And if it does happen, what then? Deal with it then, not now, when it hasn't even happened yet! And this is what we as 'normal' human beings experience on a daily basis – decision paralysis. We are so busy figuring out all of the possible connotations and consequences and outcomes of our actions that we end up doing...

N-O-T-H-I-N-G.

Because we have spent so long deciding, planning, weighing the options, that we miss the boat, and file the experience under 'Another Missed Opportunity'. And then get to 30 years old, 35 years old, 40, 47 and think, *'I wish I had done that when I had had the chance...'*

It's a condition I suffer from an awful lot in a lot of areas in my life, even down to the books I read. I have so many books that I want to read, that I cannot decide which ones to start with and so I end up reading a book I have already read, because I am constantly thinking about all the new books that I want to read, that I settle for one I know I will enjoy. And I am the 'normal' one in our relationship!

As with most of these lessons though, Tiddles doesn't wait.

He goes with it NOW.

He reacts and acts Now.

If there is something that he does have to wait for, a holiday for example, or a new DVD to be released, or whatever it may be, then he will put it into the back of his mind, and then proceed to forget about it until the time comes. He doesn't think about what might happen, and he doesn't let what happened before influence his decisions.

So Don't Wait...

Unless it's at a pedestrian crossing...

Don't waste your time with idiots

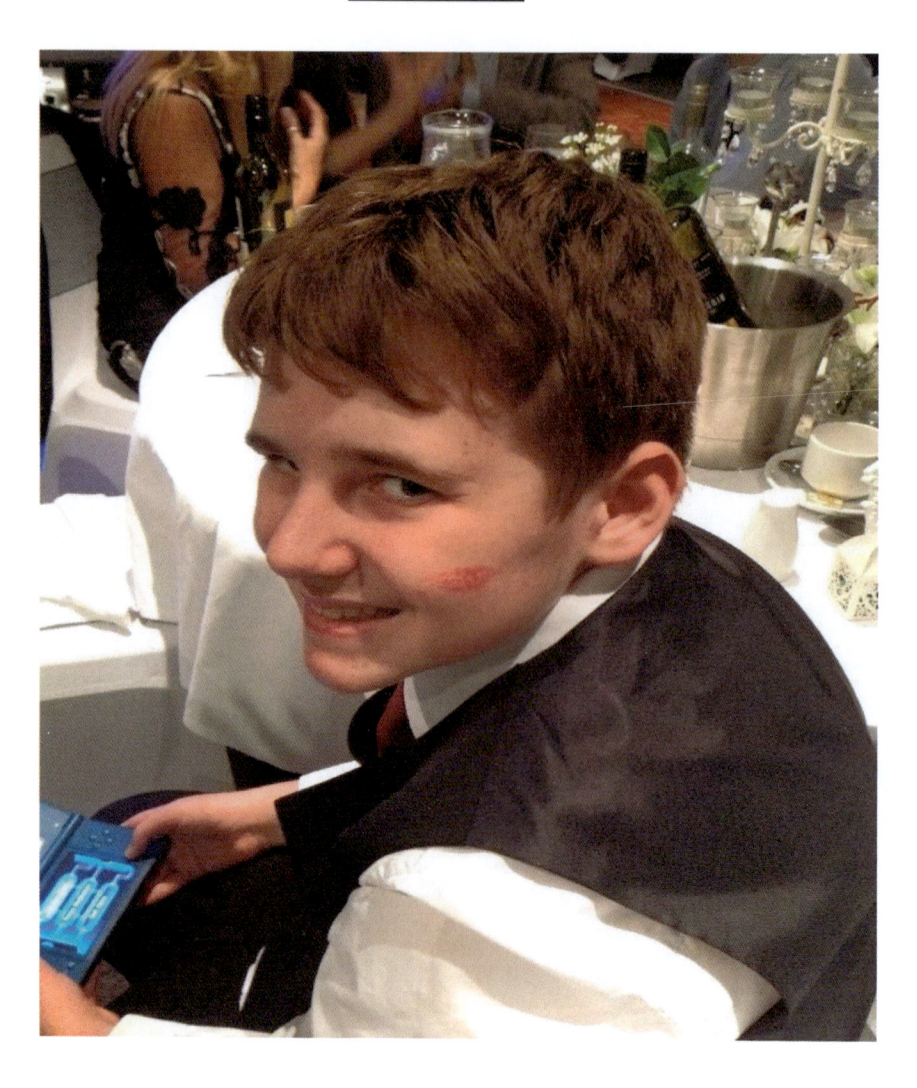

Tiddles thinks I'm an idiot. He's never actually said that, but it's there to see. He spends the bare minimum of time with me whenever he feels the need to connect. Now this could be something in his head, some synapse connection that says to him to do this, who knows? The point is that as far as he is concerned, I'm an idiot and somebody that he doesn't need to waste too much time and energy on. Which is sad (for me) and great, because already he is getting his priorities straight. Who amongst us doesn't have people or things in our lives that we continue to do just because it's something that we have always done? I know I have. We are so afraid of what others may say if we dared to change something, that we would rather keep the status quo (Latin, as opposed to the band) than actually do something else that might make us happy. And there's that word again. Happy. We can't hold it, or see it. We can only feel it, and sometimes it's reflected in our faces and our body language – we are happy. We feel happy.

And if there's one thing that I think Tiddles is, is happy.

Why?

Because he spends as little time with idiots and does the things that make him 'happy'. What a life lesson that is, if only we could follow it through.

Avoid the idiots. Don't waste your precious time and energy with people and things that make you unhappy, or bored.

Be like Tiddles.

Be Happy with who you are

Tiddles was a lovely slim little baby up until the age of 12. Then he got a bit on the chunky side. Then he slimmed down again, and now he is a little stocky again.

Does he care? He couldn't care less, to be honest.

How wonderful. How absolutely brilliant. Somebody that isn't obsessed with Body Image, unlike his father...whoever he is...(I do love that joke).

Never has Tiddles looked at somebody and thought, *'Jesus, he/she has put on a few pounds since I last saw them...'* Never going to happen. Why? Because not only is somebody's appearance unimportant to him, but he is perfectly happy in his own body. He is more than happy to stroll around with as little on as possible, and it doesn't matter who comes to visit, you're just going to have to accept the fact that this is his house, and if the sight of a teenager in a pair of underpants and a t-shirt is disturbing to you, then you know where the door is. Just another lesson that he, in his own unique way, is attempting to teach his old man.

'Look Dad, or whoever you are. You're putting yourself through all this strict diet and workout rubbish, when you could be enjoying yourself and your life a lot more if you could just let go a bit more and not be so rigid...'

And there it is...My son. He is the ultimate surfer dude, the Zen Master of Autistic philosophy. He is Patrick Swayze in 'Point Break', without the Skydiving, or Keanu Reeves. Or the bank robbing...

<u>And now...</u>

So, there you are. Life lessons that a 16 year old Autistic is trying to teach his late 40's dad, who is supposed to be full of wisdom and knowledge, but actually when it comes down to it, knows very little at all.

And do you know what? That's not entirely a bad thing.

I may not be able to teach him very much, although I did teach him to swim, to ride a bike, to read to a certain extent. But what I lack in imparting Fatherly Wisdom to him, I make up in other ways, perseverance being one.

He may not 'love' me. He may not even like me, to be honest. And that is heartbreaking for me. But whilst I hate how he is with me, I love being in his life, no matter how irritating that may be for him, because – although he'll never say it, due to his condition – he needs me.

And I want to be here. I want to keep plugging away to keep him in my life as much as possible. And in return, he is teaching me how to be a better person, a better man.

Who knows? Maybe eventually even a better father.

I wish you well.

With love,

Danson Thunderbolt.

Want to find out more about Living With Luke?

Visit the Facebook page
www.facebook.com/LivingWithLuke

Or Twitter @dansthunderbolt

There is also a play based on the blogs which has a Facebook page. For more information about it go to;
www.facebook.com/livingwithluketheplay

Printed in Great Britain
by Amazon

37826513R00027